Hazelnuts of Grace

Selections from Julian of Norwich

DEEP IN A
THOUGHTS NUTSHELL

Hazelnuts of Grace

Selections from Julian of Norwich

Compiled by Ellyn Sanna

ANAMCHARA BOOKS

Hazelnuts of Grace: Selections from Julian of Norwich

Compiled by Ellyn Sanna

Anamchara Books
220 Front Street
Vestal, NY 13850

9 8 7 6 5 4 3 2

ISBN: 978-1-937211-10-3
ebook ISBN: 978-1-937211-11-0

Library of Congress Control Number 2011909475

Cover design by Micaela Sanna.
Interior design by Camden Flath.
Printed in the United States of America.

All selections within this book are taken from *All Shall Be Well: Revelations of Divine Love*, which contains the complete book of the revelation of Julian of Norwich, written in modern language by Ellyn Sanna, available from Anamchara Books.

Contents

Introduction   7

I. The Divine One   11

1. Divine Immanence   13

2. Divine Love   23

3. The Divine Trinity   31

4. Divine Motherhood   35

5. Christ, the Divine Incarnation   43

6. The Divine Redemption of All Creation   47

II. Human Life   53

1. Human Nature   55

2. Sin   79

3. This Life's Troubles   107

4. Our Emotions   113

5. Death & Eternal Life   119

III. The Spiritual Life   125

1. Yearning & Seeking for God   127

2. Prayer   133

3. Detachment & Humility   145

4. Faith & Trust   149

IV. The Meaning of Julian's Vision   157

Introduction

The woman known today only as Julian of Norwich was born in late 1342, and she died around 1412. During these decades of the Middle Ages, the plague swept through England three times; by the time she was a young woman, she had seen many in her community succumb to the Black Death. Survivor guilt may have been what drove her to pray for suffering and sickness.

At any rate, in May 1373, when Julian was thirty-one, she became sick enough that a priest was called to administer the last rites. While she lay on what she thought was her deathbed, she had a series of intense mystical revelations. She called them "showings."

Shortly after this experience, she recovered from her illness. At some point in her life, she became an anchoress, committed to a life of prayer and meditation while confined to a cell adjoining a church. Anchoresses—women who chose to be imprisoned for God—were an accepted part of medieval life, serving a function rather like a counselor or psychologist might today. Although they had chosen a living burial, dying to the world in a very practical way, these women continued to be active in their communities. Both nobility and commoners, rich and poor, would have come to Julian's window, seeking her advice and guidance.

Julian's life as an anchoress gave her plenty of time to ponder the revelations she had received—and then write them down. She wrote in the ordinary English of her day (rather than the Latin normally used by the educated upper classes for writing), because she believed her revelations were meant to be passed along directly to all people.

It is with this in mind that Anamchara Books published *All Shall Be Well*, a modern paraphrase of Julian's text, using words that are as ordinary and accessible as possible, in order to present her meaning more clearly to all twenty-first–century readers.

The entire book deserves to be read—but it is not light reading! The selections in *Hazlenuts of Grace* are taken from

All Shall Be Well and arranged thematically in order to offer modern readers still another alternative. Each bite-size thought is intended to be read slowly, one at a time, and pondered. This is the sort of book that's meant to be picked up for five minutes and put down again, while a kernel of truth lingers in your mind throughout the day.

Julian's most famous image from her vision is the hazelnut, the tiny thing that contained within it all Creation. In a similar way, it is our prayer that you find contained in each of the small selections included here the entire depth and breadth of Julian's amazing message: *Absolutely everything will be exactly as it should be—all shall be well—because God's love sustains our world.*

I
The Divine One

God is the Ground and the Essence,

the Teaching and the Teacher,

the End and the Reward.

1

Divine Immanence

God is everything that is good.

The Spirit lives in everything good we encounter,

the entire universe,

and we shall never be abandoned.

The Divine Spirit is everything that comforts us and give us pleasure. This Spirit is our clothing. In love, the Divine One wraps us up, holds us tight, and encloses us with tenderness.

The Divine One has made and loves all reality. This is the Body, and when a human being loves others in that Body, she is loving all Creation. Contained within redeemed humanity is everything—all Creation and its Maker—for God is in humanity, and God is in all, and so everything is united into a single Body.

Just as our bodies are clothed with fabrics; our blood and muscles covered with skin; our bones wrapped with blood and muscles; and our hearts hidden at the center of all these—so are we, soul and body, clad in the goodness of God, completely enclosed and safe.

Our clothing, our flesh, our very bones,

all may grow old and waste away—

but the goodness and unity of God

are always whole and strong.

I saw God contained in a tiny particle,

a Point so infinitesimal it could barely be seen

and yet it contained the origin

and essence of all things.

God is the Midpoint of all things,

the center on which the world turns....

The Point I saw was all reality, and it contained ...

no separation from God

or the love that sustains the world.

All that exists was made by God, and so, in essence, all actions are God's doing. It is easy to understand that good deeds—what we consider to be high and moral actions—are well done, but from God's perspective, the highest level of action and the lowest are equally well done. For God has ordained the Divine Essence in each thing that exists, and all actions are simply a going forth of that Essence. And that is why there is no Doer but God.

God is the only Verb,

the single Action that moves

through every human and earthly deed.

"I complete all things,

leading them to the goal

I have ordained for them without any beginning,

by the same strength, wisdom, and love

through which I created them.

How can anything be wrong with the world,

when all this is the case?"

God *is* reality…

the substance of all things flows out from God

to work the Divine Will.

The same sacred strength, wisdom, and love that created the world also continue to work within all Creation, bringing each and every thing to God. In good time, we shall be able to see the reality of this. The Divine Essence fits all things together perfectly and sweetly; it is the substance of reality, the essence of all that is.

For God does not hold back from a single aspect of Creation, nor does the Divine One disdain to serve us in the simplest and most ordinary ways. Think how neatly our food is contained within our bodies, digested, and then is emptied out as needed, like a lovely drawstring purse that opens and closes. God is completely comfortable with all our bodies' activities; none of them offend the Divine Presence, for all our bodies' natural functions are Divine vehicles, filled with the love God bears us whose souls are made in the Divine likeness.

We are most wholly joyful

when we see God in all things.

Our most primal substance

springs from God.

Some portion of the Divine Essence lives in many forms in many creatures, and it is expressed fully in human beings, in strength, beauty, and goodness, in nobleness and dignity, in majesty, worth, and honor.

For Nature—all that has been born into life—is good and beautiful. Nature went out from God, and then grace was sent out to bring Nature back home and destroy all that would undo it, to bring Nature back to the holy Point—God—from which it first came, even more noble and worthy now, because of grace, than it was in the beginning.

Nature and grace are in agreement,

for grace is God, and Nature is God.

God works in two ways,

but Divine love is united and singular.

Nature and grace cannot be separated;

they work together.

2
Divine Love

Our beginnings

sprang from God's love.

The endless love of the Divine Essence

is also without beginning;

it continues on at this moment,

and shall exist forevermore.

God loved us before we were made, and when we were made, we loved God. This love is made out of the Holy Spirit's substance and nature, made purposeful by the strength of God the Parent, and made wise by the vision of God the Child. At the same point where our souls spring to life, created by God from God, there we are sewn tight to God.

I heard our Protector say, His voice full of joy, "My darling, look and see your Protector, your God who is your Maker and your endless joy, see what satisfaction and delight I take in your safety and wholeness. Rejoice, My love, with Me."

Mercy is an act of compassion that expresses God's Mother-hood, the Divine Feminine who is tender and loving, while grace is an act of Fatherhood, the masculine and kingly action that affirms our worth. Mercy shelters us, brings us to life, endures all pain, and heals us with infinite tenderness and love. Grace lifts us up, gazes at us with pride, and fulfills our desires with an abundance that is more than we deserve, spreading through our lives the plentiful generosity of God's royal protection and amazing courtesy. This is love's plenty, its largeness.

Mercy and grace
are two expressions of a single love.

I saw completely and certainly

that before we were ever made, we were loved.

We began to exist when God created us—but Divine love for us has no beginning. God never began to love humanity; just as human beings are intended for endless bliss, fulfilling God's joy that flows through creation, so in exactly the same way, humanity was always known by God and always loved, without any beginning. The intent of Christ, the Holy Go-Between, was always aimed directly toward this goal of endless love. The Trinity was in agreement with this intention, their Divine "Yes" spoken from before the beginning of time. The Go-Between is the Founder of the human family, the Source of our nature and life, from whom we all spring, the Womb that encloses us all. We shall all wind our way into this Go-Between, finding there our total Heaven, our everlasting joy, just as the Trinity intended all along.

Christ Himself is the basis of all human laws; He taught us to do good in the face of harm. He is Himself love, and He treats us the same way He teaches us to treat others. He wants us to be like Him, complete and whole in an endless stream of love toward ourselves and those who also follow Him.

God's love creates in us such a unity
that we cannot separate ourselves
from each other.

When grace allows us to look into the amazing Divine Goodness, we see we are endlessly made one with God in love and it is impossible that anger separate us from Divine Love. For wrath and friendship are opposite forces. How could the One who erases and heals our angry arrogance, making us gentle and humble, be anything but unified in love, all gentleness and humility, which is the opposite of wrath?

Our lives are grounded

and rooted in love;

without love,

we would not be alive.

Everything—all that exists—

draws its being from God's love.

The Spirit showed me a tiny thing the size of a hazelnut, as round as a ball and so small I could hold it in the palm of my hand. I looked at it in my mind's eye and wondered, "What is this?" The answer came to me: "This is everything that has been made. This is all Creation." It was so small that I marveled it could endure; such a tiny thing seemed likely to simply fall into nothingness. Again the answer came to my thoughts: "It lasts, and it will always last, because God loves it."

God's love for us has never diminished,

and it never will.

In this love, all Creation was made

and continues to function;

in this love, all things work out for our good;

and in this love,

we shall live forever.

3

The Divine Trinity

The essence of our being is complete

in each Person of the Trinity,

who is one God.

These three properties are at work in the Trinity:

the Fatherhood,

the Motherhood,

and the Protection—

all One God.

The Almighty Father keeps our natural substance, our sense-self, safe and joyful, as it was always, without beginning or end. Meanwhile, the Second Person's intelligence and wisdom keeps our eternal souls alongside our sense-souls, restoring us and rescuing us, for Christ our Rescuer is both our Mother and our Brother. Our good Protector, the Holy Spirit, watches over us and makes our lives and labor worthwhile, surpassing all we could desire, for the Spirit's graciousness and courtesy is amazing, exalted, and bountiful.

Our entire life is threefold: in the first aspect, we have our being; in the second, we have our growth; and in the third, we have our fulfillment. The first is our nature, the second mercy, and the third grace. The Trinity's high strength is our Father; the Trinity's deep wisdom is our Mother; and the Trinity's great love is our Protector. These Three are ours, woven into the nature and substance of our being.

We have our being in the Father, God Almighty; while we are remade and restored in our Mother of Mercy, made whole and perfect; and all the while we are fulfilled in the Spirit's grace, as we yield ourselves to our Protector. The substance of our being is in our Father, God All-Strong, and it is in our Mother, God All-Wisdom, and it is in our Protector, the Holy Spirit, God All-Goodness.

Our High Father, God All-Strong who is Being, knew and loved us before time existed. This Divine knowledge, alongside a deep and amazing love, chose with the foreknowledge of the Second Person of the Trinity to become our Mother. This was our Father's intention; our Mother brought it about; and our Protector the Holy Spirit made it firm and real. For this reason we love our God in whom we have our being.

We thank and praise our Father for our creation;

we pray with our entire intellects to our Mother

for mercy and understanding;

and we ask our Protector the Holy Spirit

for help and grace.

4

The Divine Motherhood

Through the Divine Mother,

grace is spread out wide and long,

deep and high,

like a blanket that has no edges or binding.

The High God, Sovereign Wisdom, put on flesh and mothered us in all things.

I saw that the Second Person of the Trinity is the Mother of both our eternal essence and our sense-soul. God made us with a dual nature—both a spiritual and a sense-based being. The spiritual essence is the higher part of our nature, given to us by the Father, God Almighty, nurtured in us by our Mother, the Second Person of the Trinity, in whom we are grounded and rooted. The Second Person is a merciful Mother who shares our sense-based nature and keeps our duality united and whole. In Mother Christ we are nurtured so that we grow, and in Mother Christ's mercy we are reshaped, restored, reunited with our spiritual essence, through the power of Christ's Endurance, Death, and Resurrection. This is our Mother's work in all of us who yield ourselves to Christ.

Jesus is our True Mother, the Mother of our human nature, that which we were created to be—and Jesus is also our True Mother by grace, because He chose to take on our human nature. All the qualities of motherhood come from the Second Person of the Trinity, where we are kept whole and safe, both in our human nature and by spiritual grace, fed by Christ's particular goodness.

I understood that we can consider God's Motherhood from three perspectives: the first is that the Divine Mother gave birth to us and gave us life; the second is that She shared our lives; and the third is that She works always to keep us safe. And all is one love.

> The Motherhood of mercy and grace
>
> restores us to our true natures,
>
> that which we were made to be
>
> by the Motherhood of love,
>
> the Motherhood of Being.

No one else could mother us the way Christ does.
Christ's labor pains were suffered on the Cross,
where we were birthed into joy.

A mother's help is the most intimate, the most quick to respond, and the most certain: most intimate, because it is tied to our simplest biological natures; the most quick to respond, for a mother's love is an automatic and instinctive aspect of her being; and most certain, because it lacks all artifice or pretension. Our human mothers bore us into a world of pain and death—but our True Mother, Jesus—All-Love—bears us into joy and endless life. (Blessed may She be!) In this way, Mother Christ supports and holds us in love within Herself (as a pregnant mother holds her unborn child).

Any natural, loving mother knows and understands her child's needs; she watches out for the child with vigilant tenderness. As the child grows, the mother's care changes but not her love. At some ages, the mother may allow the child to experience pain so that the child will grow in maturity and grace. In the same way, our Protector works in us. Christ is the Mother of both our human nature, our sense-selves, and our spiritual being, and sometimes our sense-selves must suffer so that our spiritual beings grow. Our Mother wants our love to be focused on Her.

Motherhood is the essence of natural love,

wisdom, knowledge—

and motherhood is God.

When we fall, God quickly lifts us up,

leaping out into our lives

like a mother playing peek-a-boo with her child,

reassuring the baby with her touch.

But often when we realize our failure and exile, we are so terribly afraid and ashamed of ourselves that we can scarcely stand ourselves. But our kind Mother does not want us to run away from Her when we feel like this; that is the last thing She wants! Instead, She wants us to be like a hurt and frightened child who runs as fast as he can to his mother. That is how Christ wants us to respond to our own failures, saying, "Mommy, Mommy, I've made myself dirty and I'm not like You anymore, and I don't know what to do. Help me!"

The Divine Nature does good in the face of evil, and it is in this way that Jesus Christ is our truest Mother, for from Christ springs our life (as it did with our human mothers), and Christ's sheltering love follows us continually throughout our entire life. Yes, God is our Father—and yes, God is also our Mother. The Divine demonstrates this in all that exists.

God is as much in the physical process

of labor and delivery

as God is in the process

of our spiritual birth.

"I am the strength and goodness of Fatherhood;

I am the wisdom of Motherhood;

I am the light and grace that comes from all true love;

I am the Trinity; I am Unity;

I am the authority of goodness living in all things.

I am the One who makes you love;

I am the One who makes you yearn for more;

and I am the endless fulfillment of all true desires."

5

Christ, the Divine Incarnation

Out of love, God made human beings,

and that same love became a human being.

Humanity's longings and desires

were made visible in Jesus.

All human beings—we who are saved by the incarnation and effort of Christ—are the Humanity of Christ. Christ is the Head of this Body of which we are all members.

But Christ's Body, in which all of us are knit together, is not yet complete in its light and life. That is why He had always experienced, without beginning or end, the same longing and thirst He experienced when He hung from the Cross, and He will continue to thirst until the last human being has been rescued and entered into His joy.

Christ is the intelligence

that works in our spirits

with limitless brightness.

The Divine Child and Adam
are one Being.

The strength and goodness we possess is the Christ in us, while the blindness and weakness is Adam. Jesus is All-Humanity who shall be saved forever, and All-Humanity (the part of us that will be saved) is Jesus: the Love of God, all that humanity possesses of humility, strength, goodness, patience, and obedience.

For at the same time that God was fastened to our human bodies within the Virgin's womb, the Divine Essence put on our sense-soul. By this action, human beings became enclosed in God, and the Divine Essence became united with our own. In this unity, God is the perfect human being, for Christ knotted to Himself each individual and thus became the Complete Human, the essence of all humanity.

Christ is always looking at us;

our souls are constantly held in His loving, yearning gaze,

for He longs for our faces to look back at Him.

When we do, Christ's grace

shall draw out our inner faces

so that they become one with our outer faces,

unified with God and with each other,

in the true and eternal joy that is Jesus.

6

The Divine Redemption of All Creation

All shall be well,

and all shall be well,

and absolutely everything shall be well.

Christ wants us to know He not only pays attention to high and great things, things that are obvious and important, but also, equally, to small things that seem trivial, simple, and hidden. This is what He meant when He said, *"absolutely everything* shall be well."

Not even the least thing

will be forgotten.

Just as the joyful Trinity

made everything out of nothing,

so the same Trinity can make well

all that is not well.

Although some deeds appear so evil from our perspective, so hurtful and damaging that no good could possibly come from them, God does not see as we do. We look at the world's events with such sorrow and grief that our vision is clouded, and we cannot see joy. But we are thinking with human reason, a perspective that is still so limited, blind, and simple that we cannot comprehend the joyful Trinity's amazing wisdom, strength, and unity.

What seems ugly and broken

is only temporary.

Ultimately, it is an illusion.

Christ taught me to focus my attention instead on the bright and splendid fulfillment of all life—for this mending of what was broken is more pleasing to God and of infinitely more worth than Adam's sin was harmful. Our Protector wants us to pay attention to this thought: "If I have made well this most basic damage to reality, this separation that is the worst that has ever befallen Creation, then you can rest assured I will also be able to make well all other things."

Straight lines cannot be made straighter; they are without flaw. God is the essence of straightness—and each Divine action is yet another line drawn straight and true, set in place from the beginning by the heights of Divine strength, wisdom, and goodness. And just as God desires what is best for each aspect of Creation, so does the Holy Spirit lead all things straight to that goal. All that God accomplishes increases Divine joy.

God makes God happy!

In Heaven, all the souls who were bent and broken will be made permanently straight in God's eyes by the power of Divine Goodness.

Our souls are made one with God who is unchangeable goodness, and so nothing exists between God and our souls, not anger, not forgiveness, for we are so completely united with God's Unity that nothing separates us from the Divine Essence.

We will be kept true to our real selves

and to God

forever and ever.

II
Human Life

We are enclosed in the Divine,

and the Divine is enclosed in us.

1

Human Nature

Our truest essence is in God.

And then our Protector opened my spiritual eyes and showed me my soul in the middle of my mind. The soul was large, an endless world, a kingdom of delight, a city of great worth. In the center of the city sat our Protector Jesus, both God and Human, a tall, beautiful Person, highest Watcher over the realm, most joyous and solemn King, worthiest Protector, clad in glory.

I saw in this vision the satisfaction and fulfillment Christ finds in the human soul. God the Creator, God the Child, and God the Holy Spirit all worked to create humanity's soul, and it was created perfectly. The Trinity takes endless joy in the human soul.

The Divine knows that which best suits God,

and the human soul suits God endlessly

and without beginning.

We can never clearly know our own souls

until we fully know God.

Through all this I saw that it is easier for us to come to know God than it is for us to know our own souls. For our souls are rooted so deeply in God, where they are so endlessly treasured, that we cannot truly know them until we first know God, the Soul-Maker, with Whom our souls are united.

If we want to understand our own selves,

if we spend time communing with our souls

and enjoying them as a lover enjoys her beloved,

it makes sense that we also seek the Divine Protector,

in Whom our souls are enclosed.

What is a soul? These visions showed me that our spiritual essence can be rightly called our soul—but at the same time, our sensual natures are also our soul. This is because of the unity they have in God; we may see them as two separate things, but they are not. Our Protector Jesus sits in the home-stead of our sense-soul, where He is enclosed, and all the while our natural essence is enclosed in Jesus, while the Soul of Christ sits at rest within the Divine Essence.

God has made us shine.

We are truly that which God loves…

because of the great riches, excellence, and abilities

given to our souls and knotted to our bodies.

These knots are what make us sense-creatures (beings who perceive reality through our senses). The human soul was made from nothing; that is to say it was brought into being from nothing that had previously been created. When God made the human body, however, the Divine Hand used the Earth's clay, solid matter that is a mixture of all the tiny pieces that make our world. So we are both Nature-made—and at the same time, we are not-made. And what is the only thing that is not-made? God! That is why God truly lives in each human soul, with nothing between the Divine Essence and ours.

In our truest essence we are complete,

even while our sense-souls fail.

No part of our nature shall die, for the highest aspects are tied to God from the time they were made, and meanwhile God is fastened to the lower aspects of our natures from the moment of our conceptions (the moment when our souls took flesh), and thus through Christ, the two aspects of our natures are united.

God's highest creation is humanity, and humans find in Christ our fullest essence and ultimate strength. Our souls are knit tightly to God at the deepest level of their being, with a knot so delicate and strong that our souls become one with God, made endlessly whole and clean and safe. God wants us to know that all souls kept safe everywhere are eternally rescued by this same knot, made one in this unity, made whole and healthy through Divine health.

Our souls were created to be God's home; and our souls' home is God, who was never created. God who is our Maker lives in our souls, and our souls live in the Divine Essence, the very substance from which we were created. Thus, I can see no difference between the Divine Essence and our own: all is God. Yet let's be clear: only God is God, and our essence is a Divine creation that lives within God.

A person can regret the pain of an experience at the same moment that she fully accepts it with all the power of her will. This paradox—two opposite feelings at one and the same time—is merely the expression of two aspects of our nature, the one our external ego and the other our inner spirit. The ego is mortal; it experiences pain and sorrow, and that is just the way things will always be in this life.

I learned the reality of selfhood: the inner spirit can be mistress of the ego. The ego does not disappear, of course, but the spirit need not pay much attention to its complaints. Instead, the spirit's will is fixed on becoming one with our Protector Jesus. I can only say what I saw—and I saw that the ego does not direct the spirit, but the spirit is capable of directing the ego.

"I will smash your empty desires,

your unhealthy selfishness—

and after that, I will gather you together,

completely clean, completely whole,

made one with Me."

In the end, both our outer and inner selves

will be united in joy

by the grace and strength of Christ.

In each soul God saves is a God-like piece, a volition that never said yes to separation from God and never will. Just as there is a selfish, lower piece in us all that wills separation and dis-unity, so there is also a higher piece that wants only good.

God assesses humanity's worth based on our nature-substance, which is always kept unified in the Divine, endlessly whole and safe. The condition of our nature-substance is protected by God's unbending goodness, from which it was made.

We have been redeemed in love,

set free from all that would make us less than we are called to be.

In the temporal life we experience here on Earth,

our sense-souls seldom know what our true selves are.

But as human beings, we judge ourselves by looking at our changeable sense-souls, which seem like one thing this minute and another thing the next, depending on what we are paying attention to (whether the high things of life or the low), and these sense-souls are what we show the outside world. The perceptions of our sense-souls are a mixed bag, because we focus on so many different things. Sometimes life seems good and easy, other times hard and painful.

All-Human's selfhood had suffered a terrible blow, as though a battering ram had slammed against him. That which had made him most strong was struck down, so that he became weak; his intellectual insights were deadened and diminished, so that he could no longer see the presence of his mistress. And yet all the while, his mistress saw his intentions as whole, and for this his mistress praised him. In himself, he had no sense of his own intentions; he was separated both from his mistress and, in a sense, from himself, so that he could not perceive the same reality the mistress saw.

When we truly see both God and ourselves,

then we shall find rest and peace.

Our truest nature and God's grace make us yearn

to know our selves in the perfection

and completion of endless joy.

But when we truly and clearly see and know our own selves, then we will truly and clearly see and know our Protector God in the fullness of joy. That is why the nearer we are to our true bliss, the more we long for it, both because of our innate natures and because of God's grace. In this life we can only know the true self by continually using the power of our higher natures. And as we come to know the true self, we can exercise it and grow, as mercy and grace pushes us forward along the straight lines that lead to God—but we can never completely know the self until we reach that ultimate point where all lines meet, the point where this passing life and all pain and sadness reach their end.

We will only know that we are blissfully safe, possessing an endless joy, when we totally rest in peace and love, completely satisfied with God and the Divine Action at work in the world, at peace with our own selves and with all who God loves, loving our own selves and all who God loves, which is what Divine love wants for us. This is what the Divine's sweet unity accomplishes in us.

When we are at peace with ourselves,

we find we have become one with God.

For in God there is nothing that is not peace.

The essence of who we are,

the very substance of our identities,

is in God, and God is in our sense-souls.

Our souls grow with our bodies, and our bodies with our souls, each lending support to the other, until we are mature, as our natures dictate. And then, as we continue to grow, rooted in the soil of this world, nourished with Divine mercy, the Holy Spirit breathes into us the gifts that lead us to endless life.

Because of the treasure of unity that God made between our souls and our bodies, humankind shall be restored out of double death into life. This restoration could not be complete without the Second Person of the Trinity taking on the physical substance of humanity's nature, which is based on the perceptions of our five senses, while at the same time our highest essence had been made one with God from the moment of creation. These two aspects of humanity are in Christ, both the higher and the lower: a single Soul. The higher-self lives always in peace with God, in complete joy and delight, while the lower-self, the sense-based nature, suffers on the Cross for humanity's redemption.

The Divine Being is nearer to us than our own souls,

for God is the soil in which our souls are rooted;

God is the Midpoint that unites

our eternal substance and our sense-souls,

so they can never be separated.

For our souls sit at rest in God;

our souls stand up straight in God's strength;

and our souls' very natures are rooted in God's endless love.

The Divine touch on the soul
is not something out of the ordinary;
it is grounded in the very nature of our being.

Our intelligence is rooted in God, the substance of our truest nature, and from our nature, mercy and grace spring and spread through us, accomplishing in our lives the fulfillment of our joy. This is the soil in which we grow and become complete.

Our primary gifts are properties of human nature, for when we were first made, God gave all these properties to our natural substance. And then the Divine Being gave us still greater purpose, for God's endless wisdom wanted us to be double beings, with twofold natures. The space created by our sense of separation from ourselves is the space where mercy and grace grow.

Our souls can never be at rest so long as they seek their comfort from things whose value is less than their own. The self is higher than all Creation, and yet we can never see our selves for very long; instead, when we look at our selves, we see the Divine, our Creator, living within us. For in the human soul is God's truest dwelling place. The light that shines from the City of the Self is the splendor of our Protector's love.

God made humanity's soul to be the Divine City,

the Home of God,

the place most pleasing to God of all Creation.

At the exact point where our souls

are connected to our flesh and senses,

at that same point God built the Divine City,

the Divine Home, a resting spot God never leaves.

God never departs from our souls;

the Divine Essence lives there with eternal joy.

It is God's delight to make the Divine Kingdom within our intelligence; to repose at rest within our souls; and to dwell there endlessly, so that we all function within God, our actions making us God's helpers as we pay attention to God, . . . desire that all actions be God's actions, and truly place our trust in God.

The Divine Essence—greatest strength, highest wisdom, deepest unity and sweetness—effortlessly guides Heaven and Earth and all that is, and makes everything bud with life. But the place that Jesus takes in our souls is unique, unviable; it can never be removed.

He finds in us His most comfortable home,

His endless dwelling place.

In God's endless love,

our souls are kept whole.

This is what all the showings demonstrated, this is what they each meant. In this endless love we are led, kept safe in God, and we will never be lost, for our safety is inherent in the moment and method of our creation. God wants us to be aware that our souls are alive, filled with life that shall endure without end, thanks to God's goodness and grace. In Heaven, we shall endlessly love God, thank God, praise God. And just as our lives will have no end, in God we were treasured and hid, known and loved, without any beginning.

What are we humans? And here is my answer: if everything in us that was not united with God was taken away, we would be completely whole. When our state of exile is taken away, then all that is left is our union with the Divine. Humans and God are one.

The soul that looks at God becomes like God,

and is united with God's rest and peace.

2
Sin

Sin is exile and separation from God.

In this stark, unadorned word—sin—our Protector brought to my mind all that is not good: the malice and total negation of all He was, the pain He bore for us in this life; His death, and all the spiritual and physical pain and suffering of His creatures. (For we are all partially negated—our full and real identities are being destroyed—and we shall be even more negated as we follow Jesus, until we are made totally whole, completely pure, with all death washed away from our bodies and all that is selfish purged from our inner selves.)

All action is God,

and sin is no action at all.

God is all reality,

and sin is the absence of reality.

Sin has no substance, no being.

In effect, it does not exist,

for it can only be known through the pain it causes.

This pain, as I understand it, is something that purifies us, that teaches us about ourselves, and that makes us rely on God's mercy.

Because our good Protector loves us so tenderly, He is quick to comfort, saying, "Granted, sin has caused you all this pain, but all shall be well, and all shall be well, and absolutely everything shall be well." These words were said with so much love, with no hint of blame. So if God does not blame me for my sin, I would be rude to blame Him for it! We are a family, connected by intimate bonds, and guilt and blame have no part in such a relationship.

We should not focus on others' sins either. Instead, we should seek God's healing and strength on behalf of us all, and when we look at another who has fallen into sin, we should focus only on compassion and our own brokenness, longing for God's healing for us both. Without this attitude, our own souls will trip and stumble into sin. Compassion is our protection.

Thinking about sin,

whether our own or another's,

creates a spiritual fog

that robs from us the sight of God's beauty.

Although I do nothing but sin,

my sin will do nothing to stop the action of God's goodness.

Whenever in this life we foolishly turn our thoughts to self-condemnation, our Protector God touches us gently, getting our attention, calling us with joy, speaking to our souls: "Let love fill you, My dear and valuable child. Turn to Me—I am enough for you—and take joy in your Rescuer and in your safety and wholeness."

Sin is the sharpest scourge that can smite any soul; it is like a knife that scrapes off our skin, a whip that beats us to the point that we look hateful to ourselves, so that afterward we think we are good for nothing but to be buried in hell. And there we sink, until our bruises become the Holy Spirit's touch on our souls, and then sin's bite sends us leaping forward into God's mercy.

Separating ourselves from God

is the most pain we will ever experience.

The Holy Spirit leads us to confess our sins,

to reveal them in all their nakedness and truth,

with such sorrow and shame

that we have dirtied God's image in our souls.

With deep tenderness, our Protector keeps us, even when it seems to us that we are forsaken, as though we have been thrown out in the garbage because of our sin, just as we feel we deserve. The gentleness and humility that comes to us from this experience raises us in God's sight; our bruises give us compassion for others and a sincere longing for God. When we reach that point, we are suddenly delivered from sin and from pain, taken up into Heaven, and transformed into saints.

God views sin as a lover looks at his beloved's sorrow and pain; out of love, God puts no mark of blame on those who sin. The consequence of sin is not insignificant, but it is high, full of light, life, and worth for us all. And so shall shame be transformed into greater worth and deeper joy.

Our kind Protector does not want us to despair no matter how often or how badly we fall, for our failures do not get in the way of Divine love.

Peace and love are always in us,

living and working,

but we do not always experience peace and love.

Christ touches us individually, in the private depths of our minds, and shows us our sin by the sweet light of mercy and grace. But when we see the pus and decay in our souls, we believe God is angry with us because of our sin. Then the Holy Spirit stirs our minds to life, our bruised souls turn to prayer, and we long with all our strength to put right our lives. We feel God is angry with us, and our feelings of guilt continue until our souls begin to find rest and our consciences grow easier. At that point, we hope God has forgiven our sins. And God has!

Our considerate and kind Protector reveals the Divine Presence to our souls; this Presence comes to us with laughter and a glad face, with a friendly welcome as if we had just come home after a painful prison sentence, saying, "My darling, I'm so glad you have finally come home to Me! In all your sadness, I was always with you, but now at last you see My love and we are united in joy."

There is no deeper hell than sin.

In fact, for the soul

that is in its natural state of connectedness with God,

there is no hell at all except for sin.

In the event that anyone is foolish enough to think that because we are offered all this spiritual comfort, we should go ahead and sin—or that we are less guilty—be careful! This is not the truth; these thoughts are the enemy of the true love that teaches us to hate sin.

Human beings are changeable while they live in this earthly life; because of their weakness and vulnerability they sometimes separate themselves from God. They are frail; they lack wisdom and insight; and their wills are easily swayed. On Earth, humanity lives in a storm of sorrow and pain, simply because we are blind—we cannot see God. If we could see God continually and clearly, then we would have no impulse to separate ourselves from the Divine Presence; none of our actions and desires would lead to sin.

Our sin turns us into outcasts from peace and love;

it separates us from them.

But God's face is always turned toward us.

We often lose sight of God.

We become preoccupied with selfish concerns, and everything seems wrong. Our lives are no longer aligned with
Divine joy; we feel as though our selves are at opposite poles
from God, and this total disjointedness from the Divine Will
is a part of our primal natures, rooted there by original sin.
This is what causes our pain and storms; this is what makes
us feel separated from God; and this is what yields earthly
life's spiritual and physical pains.

Mercy pays the price for our sin; it reverses what would have been the natural consequences of our separation from God. Mercy is sweet and generous, a work of love that mingles with abundant compassion. Mercy acts to keeps us safe, and mercy works to transform all that touches us into good. In love, mercy permits us to fail, and when we fail, we fall from God's presence; when we fall, we die, and this death is necessary whenever we lose sight and sense of the Divine Presence that is our life. Our failure is terrible, our fall is shameful, and our death is tragic—and yet through it all, the sweet Eye of love and compassion never ceases to gaze at us, and the work of mercy continues undiminished through it all.

For love is the foundation of mercy,

and mercy's action keep us safe in love.

Grace and mercy were one, two sides of love's face.

The Divine mercy

went with the All-Human into Hell,

and it kept him safe there.

All of us whom Christ has rescued have within us a marvelous mingling of health and wounds, wholeness and sorrow, for we contain in our beings both Jesus our Risen Protector and Adam, who fell into death. In Christ, we are kept steadfastly safe; the touch of His grace on our lives raises us into the certainty of our safety—but at the same time, we are terribly broken, our emotions and vision shattered by Adam's fall, so that we experience pain, sin, and darkness.

We hate the arrogant stirrings in our minds, all that causes us to fall away from God, physically and spiritually. But then again, we lose sight of the Divine sweetness, and we fall once more into such darkness that we stumble into all manner of sorrows and troubles. We can only comfort ourselves that we never give our deepest permission for the trouble and sorrow to enter our lives. We revolt against the darkness, our minds filled with groaning, enduring the pain and sadness, praying for the time when the Divine Presence will once again be revealed to us.

The strength of Christ our Protector

guards our inmost beings.

When we sin, we neither wallow in despair

nor do we become reckless,

treating sin as though it didn't matter;

instead, we honestly acknowledge our weakness

as we stand naked before God,

accepting that in our own strength

we cannot keep our balance for even the blink of an eye.

All we can do is humbly cling to God.

God's viewpoint is totally different from humanity's. As human beings, it is our role to search out our sins and weaknesses, examining ourselves with deep humility—but meanwhile, the role of our Protector God is to look past all our weakness, calling us upward into Divine goodness and unity. The outward reality was one of weakness and humbleness, while the inner reality was that of endless love.

This double awareness—of both our weakness and our total security in Divine love—is what our Protector asks of us, and it is this that the Divine Presence brings to life in our hearts. Both realities are true: the lower, external reality and the deeper, inner reality. Human beings have fallen into terrible darkness and pain—and all the while, they are eternally protected, their beings fulfilled in the Divine.

Once we are united with the High Self,

all our failures will be turned into an endless treasure.

In every soul kept safe by God there lives a will that never agreed to be separated from the Divine, nor ever will agree, despite the appearance of external circumstances. This aspect of the human soul is the Divine Will living in us, a sense of volition that is so good it can never say yes to the presence of evil; instead, it always leans toward goodness, and it works for the unity of all things in the sight of God. Our Protector wants us to be assured of this reality, that a piece of our very essence remains whole and safe in Jesus Christ, our Divine Protector. In Heaven, all created beings will be knit tight to God, fulfilled by the Divine alignment and unity—but this will only be possible because all along a part of our deepest substance was never separated from God, nor ever could be because of the Divine Vision, endless and unlimited, that works with the Divine Will, drawing straight lines toward the single Point where all is One.

Sin is on the furthest opposite end from all that is God,

and so long as we meddle with anything
remotely connected to sin

(as long as we allow our awareness

to be mixed together with that

which separates us from an awareness of God),

we shall never see clearly our Protector's joyful and kind face.

When we take our leave of Christ's mind within us,

neglecting to keep our souls whole—

then Christ keeps them whole by Himself,

standing guard over us with sorrow and yearning. ...

When I put myself outside of Him

because of my sin, despair, or laziness,

then I leave my Protector standing alone in my mind.

The more horrible and painful our sins, the deeper this glad sight is hidden from our vision. This is why we feel so often as though we are in mortal danger, as though we were in a region of hell, but it is only the sorrow and pain within our own minds that we feel. But we are like dead people, unable to see the reality of our own joyous life. And yet we are not dead in God's sight nor does the Divine Presence ever leave us. God's joy in us will never be complete, though, until we finally see clearly God's friendly, loving face. This is what we were made for, this is the fulfillment of our deepest natures, and grace brings us to what we were always meant to be. And this is the way that sin is deadly, but only for a short time in our lives' endless blessing.

Take constant comfort in what God told me:

"I keep you safe."

If through our weakness or blindness we fall, then our kind Protector touches us and inspires us and calls us, so that we become aware of our brokenness. But God does not want us to dwell on this awareness; the Divine will would not have us become preoccupied with accusing ourselves or being exiled from ourselves. Instead, God wants us to quickly turn back to the Divine Presence.

For we are God's

joy and delight.

We will rise up again in strength

and see God anew.

What is it in this life that separates us into two pieces? Is it evil? Or is it good? And I say, in that it serves us and helps us grow, it is good (it heals us and unites us with God)—but in that it makes us lose our sense of who we are in the Divine, it is evil. If we willfully point our minds toward this state of exile, then it is sin—and we are plunged into a state of suffering that is worse than all others. But if we hate our feelings of exile and separation from the Divine, when we are filled with love and yearning for God, then we are fine. When we sincerely feel these things, we may sin because we are weak or blind, but we still do not fall.

When we come to God through the Church, we learn to hate sin. We look back on our past sins with guilt and sorrow, and yet we continue to fall away from our promises over and over in small daily ways, failing to live in the new state of being our Protector has created for us. Then we are filled with shame and sorrow; the sight of our selves weighs us down, to the point that we can scarcely find any comfort.

We mistake this fear and guilt for humility, but it is not; it is instead a sick and ugly blindness, a weakness. We do not realize that these feelings are sin. The Enemy sends them creeping into our minds so subtly that we do not know enough to reject them the way we would other sins. They are lies, sent by the one who hates our souls.

He guides us to hold tight to Him, to fasten ourselves to Him in the most intimate way possible, forever, in whatever condition we find ourselves, whether we are clean or dirty in our own eyes, for His love for us never changes. Because we are changeable while we live in this temporary life, we fall often into sin—and then the Enemy as well as our own foolishness and blindness fill us with fear and doubt by telling us, "See what a wretched being you are, how bad you are, how unfaithful you are. You don't keep your promises. You tell Jesus you will do better, but you never do. You make the same mistakes over and over. Most of all, you're lazy and you waste time."

Whether we are well or ill, whole or broken,

Christ wants us to never run away from Him.

The soul who is focused

on the Divine Nature of our Protector Jesus

hates no hell but that which comes

when we separate ourselves from God.

When we become aware that we are broken and exiled, we flee to our Protector—and in our flight, we are healed. For the more needy we are, the more we need to touch the hem of the Divine Presence.

We need to see our sin clearly, so that we can lose our false pride and presumption, so that we understand how we have become bent from the shape God wanted for us. As our Protector shows us the smallest glimpses of this reality, we are able to throw ourselves forward toward the reality we cannot see. God is kind; we only see that which we can bear to see.

I will again and again fall into sin, and so I learned to examine myself and question myself at all times. I do not know in what ways I will fall, nor can I predict how severely I will stumble. I only know I cannot trust myself not to sin. And yet our kind Protector revealed with great certainty and strength that Divine love is endless and unchangeable. By God's great goodness and grace, we are kept safe, and we shall never be separated from love.

Love's comfort and joy

protect me from despair.

Oh Exiled One, separated from God and from your own sense of yourself! What are you? You are nothing. When I saw that God had made all things, I saw no sinners such as you. And when I saw that God is in all things, I did not see you. And when I saw that God *does* all things, both small and large, I did not see you. And when I saw our Protector Jesus in our souls—sharing His worth with us, His love, His pleasure, His authority, and all that He has made—I did not see you. And that is why I am certain that you are truly nothing. Anything that has to do with you in any way is nothing, and it shall be endlessly and totally overthrown. May God shield us from you!

Let it be so in love.

3

This Life's Troubles

Our trials are not punishments.

When we fall into storms and sorrows,

we die, as is our destiny here on Earth,

but meanwhile, in God's sight, the soul is kept safe, alive;

it is not dead, nor shall it ever be.

In the lives of all whom God loves, He allows some troubles to enter. In His eyes they have no shame, even though others may regard them with scorn, mockery, and rejection. When we are abused and violated, snatched out of our sense of who we are, we are at the same time rescued from this life's emptiness, and our path toward Heaven then lies more clearly before us.

We (who are still so foolish) feel as though we've accomplished nothing, that all our spiritual journeys have been delusions. But this is not reality. We need to fall sometimes—and we need sometimes to feel our failure. If we did not, we would not know how weak and exiled from our true selves we are, nor would we truly understand how much our Creator loves us. When we reach Heaven, we will clearly see how terribly we separated ourselves from God—and how despite that, Divine love for us never diminished nor did we ever become less precious in God's eyes.

Most of us, though, fall first and only later come to understand that we are still held safe in God's love.

Our failures and our understanding
are both contained within the mercy of God.

Our Protector wants us

to help ourselves with wide-open mouths

to as much as we can of the comfort and direction

God offers, focusing all our attention there—

while at the same time, we only nibble

at this world's troubles and discomforts

before we set them aside as insignificant.

The less we focus on them,

the less important they will feel,

and the less they will bother us.

Even in those times when we are in so much pain and distress that we cannot focus on anything but our feelings, we can rest assured that these sensations count for nothing; we can pass over them lightly, without paying much attention to them. Why? Because God wants to be in an intimate relationship with us; and if we know God, love God, and are filled with reverence and awe for God, we shall have peace. Everything God does will create in our minds an enclosed garden of joy and delight, a place where we can be safe and happy.

Our minds will be at rest.

Christ did not say,

"You'll never encounter storms,

you'll never have troubles,

you'll never be afflicted."

What He said was,

"You shall not be overcome."

4

Our Emotions

God allows us to feel a range of emotions—

but they are all expressions of Divine love.

Our souls are driven forward by the emotional cycles we all experience: sometimes we are comforted, and sometimes we feel we have been abandoned. God wants us to understand that our emotions are not reality. The Divine One keeps us equally safe in sadness and in happiness. Both sorrow and elation are God's gifts to us through our emotions.

The Divine hands are always outstretched to us

with good things God wants to give.

Despite our up-and-down feelings of sadness and happiness,

God wants us to understand and hold tight to the belief

that our being exists more in Heaven than it does on Earth.

When we experience depression and anxiety, we should not allow our minds to dwell on these feelings. Like any temporary pain, these sensations are to be endured until they pass—and then we can move on once more to the endless enjoyment God offers us.

The Trinity's three Persons—Strength, Wisdom, and Love—are all equally present in the human self, but my mind can best understand love. I believe God wants us to see and enjoy all life in the light of love. But we are ignorant and blind when it comes to this realization. Some of us believe that God is Almighty, able to do all things, and many of us believe God is All-Wisdom, able to do all things. But we stop short at believing that God is All-Love, able to do all things. This ignorance on our part is what hinders us most, I believe.

We go through so much pain in life

because we do not fully comprehend love.

God hates despair.

The Divine longs to transform this feeling in our hearts

into a knowledge of love,

and grace will do so if we rest in the knowledge

that we were created for love.

Our Protector is never pleased

when we doubt that God is good.

Though God can transform all our fears, be careful of any fear that makes you feel separated from the Divine. The only sort of fear that is truly of God is the fear that makes us flee to our Protector's breast, throwing our whole selves on God the way a child buries his head in his mother. This fears makes us aware that we are weak and needy, but only so we are driven to God's everlasting sweetness and unity, to the friendly Divine love.

The sort of fear that makes us cling to God, full of trust and confidence, is the only type of fear that is good and true, springing from grace. Fear that does not possess these qualities is a crooked sort of thing that pulls us out of alignment. Recognize the difference and refuse to allow anything that distorts the truth to take root in your mind.

5

Death & Eternal Life

You shall come higher,

into my Realm.

Suddenly you shall be taken from all your pain,

sickness, despair, and distress,

and you shall be filled with love and delight.

And then you will never again feel any kind of pain;

nothing will distress you;

no sluggishness will weaken you.

Joy and light will be yours endlessly.

Knowing this waits for you,

why should you be so upset

about this world's temporary discomforts?

Our lives will be

forever fulfilled at last.

Our Faith has always told us that when God rescues us from this life, all our pain and sorrow shall end. And not only will we receive the same friendly joy that other souls have experienced in Heaven, but we will also receive a new, unique delight all our own, which will flow without limit from God into us, filling us full. This is the heavenly merchandise God planned to give us from the beginning, the treasure God keeps hidden for us, waiting until the time when we are increased enough to be able to receive it.

When the Last Day comes,

and we are all brought up from this world,

then we shall see in God all the secrets that are now hidden.

And not one of us will want to say,

"God, if only…"

Instead, with one voice we shall say,

"Be blessed, Protector God,

for all is as it is,

and all is completely good."

The grace of the Holy Spirit calls to us, all through our lives and even as we die, filling us always with the longing to be loved. And then we will enter our Protector, and our selves will clearly know at last. We will fully have God, and God will have us, endlessly and totally. We will truly see God, fully feel God, clearly hear God. We will swallow God; we will drink God.

How sweet

is the taste of the Divine!

Our entire life,

all the weakness and dullness we experience here,

is actually only a single point

from which we shall step suddenly

into such delight that all our pain

will disappear into nothingness.

III
The Spiritual Life

God is pleased when we seek

the Divine Presence continually.

1
Yearning & Seeking for God

Longing is the road we travel,

and desire is our road map.

In this world, we are so blind and ignorant that we fail to seek the Divine Presence until It is revealed to us. As soon as we catch a glimpse of God, however, grace stirs us, and we yearn to see yet more clearly and joyfully.

And so I both saw God, and at the same time I longed to see God; I had God, even as I yearned for God. This is the way our lives go; this is the way they are meant to go while we are in this life.

From our perspective,

we do nothing but seek and suffer.

We see with clarity that we have found God

only when the Spirit's special grace reveals this to us.

It is the seeking, with faith, hope, and love,

that pleases our Protector,

while it is the finding

that pleases us and fills us with joy.

During this time that we suffer on Earth, seeking is as good as seeing. Leave your awareness of the Divine Presence up to God, in humility and trust, to reveal to you as God wants. Our only job is to cling to God with total trust. Whether we see God or only seek to see God, I believe we add to the Divine Essence when we simply fasten our minds and lives onto God.

By the strength and goodness of Christ's longing
we are drawn to Him.
Our own souls answer His with yearning;
without this, none of us would come to Heaven.

Seeking and asking

is a true, joyful, and enduring soul-quality,

a part of whom we are as human beings.

The more glimpses we get by grace of God's happy love, the more we long to see it in all its fullness. For even though our Protector God dwells in us and is here with us, even though God clasps us close and encloses us with gentle love and never leaves us and is nearer to us than tongue can tell or mind can think—yet our yearning and sorrow will never end until we at last see clearly the Divine Face in all its friendliness and joy. When we see that glad sight, we will no more sigh and sorrow. We know that all is whole, each good thing in our lives solid and unshaken.

The very nature of our souls

makes us constantly yearn with a sense of emptiness.

Even if everything comforting and good God had ever made in either Heaven or Earth were given to us, we would still be filled with spiritual sorrow if we did not see God's glad face.

Divine love makes God long for us; Divine wisdom, truth, and straightforwardness make God allow us to be here on Earth, separated in some measure from God; and God puts in us this same mixture of longing for something more while we live in what we have here on Earth. This is our natural penance, and this is the best penance, the only penance we need, for it is a part of our minds and always will be until we are fulfilled at last, when we have the Gift for which we have always longed.

2
Prayer

Prayer makes us as we should be,

stretched out straight and true toward God.

In our ignorance and incomprehension of Love, we use many methods for asking God for what we want. But I realized now that God is worshipped—and delighted—when we simply turn to the Divine One, trusting totally in that Unity and clinging to Divine grace. This attitude reveals a deeper under-standing of God and creates in us an unshakeable love, far more than any method of prayer our minds could contrive.

Even if we were to practice all the prayer techniques ever used, they would never be enough to connect our souls to God with utter wholeness and fullness, for God's goodness is the entire whole of reality, a unity that lacks absolutely nothing.

By focusing our attention here—

on the absolute Unity that never fails—

we achieve the truest form of prayer.

Resting in this Unity is the highest prayer,

and it reaches down to our deepest needs.

It brings our souls to life; it brings us more of life's fullness; and our lives expand with grace and strength. This attitude of prayer aligns most easily with our very natures, and it requires the least effort to achieve, for it is simply what our souls already crave, and what they shall always crave until we truly understand that we are wrapped in the Divine Unity: the goodness of God.

We do not make God act with our prayers,

as though we could move the Divine Essence

to be what we want,

but rather that the Divine

lives in our true desires.

"I am the Ground of each thing for which you ask. It is My will first that you have whatever it is, and then I make you yearn for it, and then you ask Me for it—so why would I not then give you that for which I have made you yearn?"

Our Protector laughs with gladness at our prayers. He takes care of them and works through them to change our lives, for Divine grace makes us like God, not only because we are connected to Christ with the bonds of family love and relationship, but because we are becoming like Him.

That is why God directs us, "Pray inside your minds, even if you feel no emotional satisfaction from doing so, for it is good for you, even if you can't feel the benefits, even if you can't see them, even if you think you are incapable of prayer. In the midst of dryness and barrenness, in your sickness and weakness, your prayers always make Me happy, even if you feel your prayer is flavorless and dry. I treasure all your prayers."

The Divine Will urges us

to pray continually.

God accepts our good intentions and our hard work, no matter how we feel emotionally. That is why we please God when we exert all our strength to pray and live united with the Divine; with God's help and grace, then, we keep all our abilities, our mental focus, our body's perceptions turned toward God, until we have what we seek, until our joy is complete, until we have Jesus.

Prayer is like an arrow

shot straight toward joy's completion in Heaven—

and prayer is also like a shelter

that covers us with the knowledge

that we can trust God to grant all for which we yearn.

If we pray and see no answer, we become weighed down with doubt, and that profits no one. But on the other hand, if we just sit back and see what God is doing and never bother to unite ourselves with the Divine Verb through prayer, then we are holding ourselves back, not investing in the work God is doing, and we diminish its action in our own minds.

Sometimes it occurs to us that we have been praying a long time and have received no answer. We should not let ourselves be weighed down with these thoughts. I am certain that what our Protector wants us to understand from this showing is that either we must wait for a better time for what we desire or we must wait for a better gift.

God knows the best match

for all our desires.

There are many times

when we cannot perceive God's presence in our lives,

and then we go to Jesus, hungry and needy,

reliant on prayer to enable us to go on.

For when storms toss our souls, when we feel lonely and troubled, then we need to pray, so that we will become pliable in God's Hand, supple and responsive to the flow of the Divine Will. (Remember, though, prayer does not shape God nor do we channel the Divine Will so that it flows in one direction or another, for God is always the same in love.)

Prayer makes the soul one with God. Our souls are like God in their essence, and they are connected to God with bonds of kinship—yet because of sin, our *way* of being is often not much like God's. That is why we need to use prayer as an affirmation that our souls are aligned with the Divine Will. What's more, prayer comforts our uneasy consciences and becomes a conduit for grace to flow into us.

For God looks at us with love; God wants to make us partners in all the good the Divine Will accomplishes; and that is why we are inspired to pray for that which pleases God.

Prayer matches our minds
to God's.

Giving thanks is a part of prayer,

a true heart-knowledge.

For our part, we must take care to always lovingly choose prayer as a way of life. We may still feel as though we have accomplished nothing—but in reality (whether we can see it or not), we have. And if we do what we can and ask with constancy and faithfulness for mercy and grace, then all that we lack we shall find in God.

When our generous and considerate Protector through grace reveals the Divine to our souls, then we have all we desire, and our prayers are struck dumb. We cannot think of any other prayer, for we are so focused on the vision of God. In my opinion, this is a mountaintop form of prayer, a prayer that lies beyond our senses and human faculties. All the strands of our requests are pulled together into a single cord: looking at the One to whom we pray, the center and focal point of all prayer. Then we are filled with marvelous joy and reverent awe, such sweetness and delight that the straight lines of our various prayers become a single point: God. And there they remain, until the Divine Will once more stirs us to prayer for the details of our lives.

Simply enjoying our Protector

is the best prayer.

3

Detachment & Humility

When we perceive the nothingness in external reality,

we find God there.

No soul finds peace

until it achieves nothingness

even in the midst of the created world.

Our minds and souls are often restless and uncomfortable, because we rely on things that are so small, which can offer us no real rest or security, while we fail to realize that God is Almighty, All-Wise, All-Good. The Divine One is the essence of rest and security, the only true comfort. God wants to be known; the Divine One is pleased when we rest in the Spirit's presence, since all that was created will never be enough in and of itself to give us what we need. When we willingly, lovingly detach our minds from the world around us, we have the One who is all—and we find rest for our spirits.

Look at the big picture rather than the small.

See Divine grace as it has been shown to you

in everything around you.

It is worth more to God

if you can perceive the Divine Presence in all life

rather than merely in any specific creation.

We should not allow ourselves

to become attached

to individual aspects of Creation,

but instead, we should enjoy

God's worth in everything.

This means as well that we

will not be greatly distressed

if we lose one aspect of life,

for we can rest in the confidence

that the whole of reality is still fine—

for absolutely everything shall be well.

4
Faith & Trust

As we trust and enjoy our Rescuer, Jesus,

we shall have everything in Him.

Our faith is a strength that the Holy Spirit brings out of our nature-substance into our sense-soul, and through this faith, all other strengths come to us. Without faith, we are weak, for faith is merely a straight and direct understanding (a true belief, a deeply rooted trust) in whom we are: that we are in God, and God—whom we cannot see—is in us.

The strength that faith yields in us

accomplishes great things,

allowing us to live as Christ's children.

God does not want us to dread that which is unknown

but instead to rest in love and joy.

Divine love is so great that it reveals to us all that we need to know, that which enriches us and makes us grow. And even that which is kept secret is still revealed to us in guarded glimpses, so that we will trust in God's endless kindness, rejoicing in all that is revealed and in all that is hidden. If we do this with determination and humility, we shall find great comfort, and we shall receive God's endless thanks.

If we do not trust as much we pray, our prayers are emptied of worth, plus we make our own lives more difficult for ourselves. This is because, I believe, we don't really comprehend that our Protector is the Ground from which our prayers spring, nor that our desires are given to us by grace, by the generosity of Christ's love. If we grasped the reality of this, we would have total confidence that God will grant all that we truly desire.

No one sincerely asks for grace and mercy

without having already been given

grace and mercy.

I believe life offers us no higher spiritual roles

than those we find in childhood.

Only when we reach the Father's glad and friendly Presence will we climb again as high as we do in childhood, even though as children, our strength and intelligence were not fully developed yet. Only children have the strength to believe—and only then shall we shall understand what Christ meant—when He said, "All shall be well, and you shall see for yourself that absolutely everything will be well." And then the joyous kindness of our Mother, in Christ, shall begin anew, a Divine joy whose beginning shall endure forever, a new beginning that never ends.

Human children trust their mother's love;

they love their mothers with humility and confidence,

just as they love the other children in the family.

Our Heavenly Mother is pleased

by these same characteristics in Her children.

Our faith is a natural light

that indicates the coming of endless day.

This light is carefully measured out to us, so that we have what we need to get through the night. This light gives us life, while the night is the cause of all our pain and sadness. God thanks us and rewards us for enduring the darkness. With mercy and grace, we hold firm, believing that our light is real, and that we can follow it with wisdom and strength.

The light is never so great that we see complete Daylight, nor is it ever kept from us so that utter darkness falls. It is just enough light for us to live as we need, with hard work and pain, so that we earn God's endless affirmation.

And when all sadness ends,

suddenly our eyes will open.

In the clear daylight, our vision will be complete.

In this way I came to understand

that our faith gives light to our night,

and that same light is God,

our endless day.

IV
The Meaning of Julian's Vision

Love was the meaning

in everything God had shown me.

"It is I, I am the One:

I am the One who is highest,

I am the One you love,

I am all that you enjoy,

I am what you serve,

I am that which you long for most,

I am all that you desire,

I am who lives in your thoughts,

I am everything."

Our lives here on Earth

are filled with touches of grace

and glimpses of Divine light,

which guide our faith on paths of hope and love,

commitment and repentance.

As we make a space in our lives

for looking at God, we will experience

all manner of comfort and happiness.

Do you really want to clearly see the Protector's meaning in the showings? Well, then, learn it well: Love was God's meaning. Who showed you these visions? Love. What were you shown? Love. Why were you shown these vision? For love. Hold on to that love, and you will learn and understand more of the same love—but you will never learn nor understand anything else.

And in love, we see God endlessly,

world without end.

This book is begun by God's gift,

by Divine grace,

but I do not believe it has yet been finished.

It is still developing and growing.

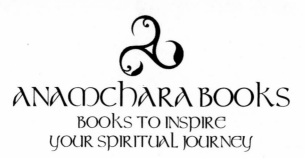

ANAMCHARA BOOKS
BOOKS TO INSPIRE
YOUR SPIRITUAL JOURNEY

In Celtic Christianity, an *anamchara* is a soul friend, a companion and mentor (often across the miles and the years) on the spiritual journey. Soul friendship entails a commitment to both accept and challenge, to reach across all divisions in a search for the wisdom and truth at the heart of our lives.

At Anamchara Books, we are committed to creating a community of soul friends by publishing books that lead us into deeper relationships with God, the Earth, and each other. These books connect us with the great mystics of the past, as well as with more modern spiritual thinkers. They are designed to build bridges, shaping an inclusive spirituality where we all can grow.

You can order our books at **www.AnamcharaBooks.com**. Check out our site to read opinions and perspectives from our editorial staff on our Soul Friends blog. You can also submit your own blog posts by emailing **info@AnamcharaBooks.com** with "Blog Entry for Soul Friends" in the subject line. To find out more about Anamchara Books and connect with others on their own spiritual journeys, visit **www.AnamcharaBooks.com** today.

ANAMCHARA BOOKS
220 Front Street
Vestal, New York 13850
(607) 785-1578
www.AnamcharaBooks.com